Animal Opposites

HEAVY
and
Light

An Animal Opposites Book

by Nathan Olson

Capstone
press

Mankato, Minnesota

Some animals are so heavy they can't jump. Others are so light they flutter in the air. Let's learn about heavy and light by looking at animals around the world.

3

HEAVY

Turkeys are heavy, plump birds.
Some weigh too much to fly.

Light

Hummingbirds are light, thin birds. They can easily zip from flower to flower.

HEAVY

The whale shark is the heaviest
fish in the world. It weighs as
much as a school bus.

Light

How light is a yellow tang fish? It weighs about the same as a golf ball.

Yellow tangs use their snouts to eat small plants from rocks.

HEAVY

Some dogs are heavy. The English Mastiff weighs about the same as a baby horse.

Light

Some dogs are light. Chihuahua pups weigh about the same as a can of soda.

HEAVY

Pythons grow thick and heavy. It takes several people to lift one.

Pythons can swallow prey as large as a crocodile.

Light

Green mamba snakes are light and skinny. They don't need to be heavy. They have a deadly bite.

HEAVY

Polar bears are heavy mammals. Their blubber keeps them warm in the cold ice and snow.

White bats are light mammals. They hang upside down from banana leaves to rest in the cool shade.

13

HEAVY

The leatherback turtle is the heaviest reptile in the world. It weighs as much as a small car.

The leatherback turtle weighs about 2,000 pounds (907 kilograms).

The dwarf gecko is the lightest reptile in the world. Some weigh less than a coin.

HEAVY

Goliath beetles are heavy insects. A single goliath beetle can weigh more than a tennis ball.

Light

Ants are light insects. But they can carry a heavy load. Ants can lift things many times their own weight.

HEAVY

Gorillas have heavy bodies. They need strong arms to help them stand and walk in the rain forest.

Light

Spider monkeys have light bodies. They swing from branches with their thin arms, legs, and tails.

HEAVY

Yaks are mountain animals covered with heavy, coarse hair.

In Tibet, yak hair is used to make tents.

Poodles are dogs covered with light, curly hair.

HEAVY

Prairie dogs that are fed
too much human food
grow fat and heavy.

Light

Light, fit prairie dogs
scamper around and
eat just enough.

23

HEAVY

Elephants are so heavy they can't even jump!

Light

Elephant nose fish are so light you can carry one home for your fish tank.

Some heavy animals weigh as much as a bus. Some light animals weigh less than a coin.

What kinds of heavy and light animals live near you?

Did You Know?

A single ruby-throated hummingbird weighs less than a nickel. It would take eight or nine hummingbirds sitting together on a scale to weigh 1 ounce (28 grams).

When goliath beetles fly, they make a noise like a toy helicopter.

The prairie dog is not a dog at all. It is a ground squirrel. These animals live in colonies or towns. Some prairie dog towns are home to more than 500 of these burrowing creatures.

Male gorillas are almost twice as heavy as female gorillas.

The polar bear is the heaviest bear in the world. Most adult male polar bears weigh between 900 and 1,500 pounds (408 and 680 kilograms).

Glossary

blubber (BLUH-bur) — the fat under the skin of a polar bear; blubber helps polar bears stay warm.

coarse (KORSS) — having a rough texture

creature (KREE-chur) — a living being

deadly (DED-lee) — able to kill

insect (IN-sekt) — a small animal with a hard outer shell, six legs, three body sections, and two antennas; most insects have wings.

mammal (MAM-uhl) — a warm-blooded animal that has a backbone and feeds milk to its young; mammals also have hair and give live birth to their young.

plump (PLUHMP) — somewhat fat or round

prey (PRAY) — an animal that is hunted by another animal for food

rain forest (RAYN FOR-ist) — a thick forest where a great deal of rain falls

reptile (REP-tile) — a cold-blooded animal with a backbone; scales cover a reptile's body.

Read More

Arps, Melissa. *Opposites.* School Days. New York: Random House Children's Books, 2006.

Bullard, Lisa. *Big and Small: An Animal Opposites Book.* A+ Books: Animal Opposites. Mankato, Minn.: Capstone Press, 2006.

Thomas, Frances. *Little Monster's Book of Opposites.* New York: Bloomsbury Children's Books, 2005.

Internet Sites

FactHound offers a safe, fun way to find Internet sites related to this book. All of the sites on FactHound have been researched by our staff.

Here's how:

1. Visit *www.facthound.com*

2. Choose your grade level.

3. Type in this book ID **142961210X** for age-appropriate sites. You may also browse subjects by clicking on letters, or by clicking on pictures and words.

4. Click on the **Fetch It** button.

FactHound will fetch the best sites for you!

Index

32

A+ Books are published by Capstone Press,
151 Good Counsel Drive, P.O. Box 669, Mankato, Minnesota 56002.
www.capstonepress.com

1 2 3 4 5 6 13 12 11 10 09 08

Library of Congress Cataloging-in-Publication Data
Olson, Nathan.
     Heavy and light: an animal opposites book / by Nathan Olson.
     p. cm. — (A+ books. Animal opposites)
     Includes bibliographical references and index.
     ISBN-13: 978-1-4296-1210-4 (hardcover)
     ISBN-10: 1-4296-1210-X (hardcover)
     1. Animals — Juvenile literature. 2. Body weight — Juvenile literature. I. Title. II. Series.
QL49.O63 2008
590 — dc22   2007036217

Summary: Brief text introduces the concepts of heavy and light, comparing some of the
     world's heaviest and lightest animals.

Credits
Heather Adamson and Megan Peterson, editors; Renée T. Doyle, designer;
     Wanda Winch, photo researcher

Photo Credits
AP Images/Penn State/S. Blair Hedges, 15; Capstone Press/Karon Dubke, 25; Creatas,
11; Digital Vision, 12, 24; iStockphoto, 3 (bottom right); iStockphoto/Frank Leung, 3
(bottom left); iStockphoto/John Pitcher, cover (polar bear); iStockphoto/Klaas
Lingbeekvan Kranen, 6–7; iStockphoto/Rick Miller, 1 (right), 27 (bottom); iStockphoto/
Timothy Wood, cover (hummingbird), 28; James P. Rowan, 12–13; Minden Pictures/Ingo
Arndt, 19; Minden Pictures/Mark Moffett, 16–17; Nature Picture Library/Bruce
Davidson, 16; Nature Picture Library/Shattil & Rozinski, 23; Peter Arnold/Ron Giling,
10–11; Peter Arnold/Rouquette F./PHONE Labat J.M., 8–9; SeaPics.com/Mark Conlin,
14–15; Shutterstock/Bruce Shippee, 26 (bottom left); Shutterstock/Christophe Testi, 7;
Shutterstock/Christopher Marin, 22; Shutterstock/Donald Gargano, 18; Shutterstock/
dvest, 26 (top); Shutterstock/Graham Taylor, 27 (top); Shutterstock/Jan Quist, 2
(bottom); Shutterstock/Kiyoshi Takahase Segundo, 5; Shutterstock/Natalia V. Guseva, 26
(bottom right); Shutterstock/Pavitra, 9; Shutterstock/Petrov Andrey, 20; Shutterstock/
Phillip Holland, 4; Shutterstock/Racheal Grazias, 21; Shutterstock/Robert Hardholt, 1
(middle), 3 (top); Shutterstock/Tim Zurowski, 1 (left); Shutterstock/Vera Bogaerts, 2 (top)

Note to Parents, Teachers, and Librarians

This Animal Opposites book uses full-color photographs and a nonfiction format
to introduce children to the concepts of heavy and light. *Heavy and Light* is
designed to be read aloud to a pre-reader or to be read independently by an
early reader. Photographs help listeners and early readers understand the text
and concepts discussed. The book encourages further learning by including the
following sections: Did You Know?, Glossary, Read More, Internet Sites, and
Index. Early readers may need assistance using these features.